Prometheus
The Sacred Devil

Abdolhai Shammasi

TSL Drama

Characters

1- YOUNG MAN - dressed in rags, cloak

2- WOMAN - middle-aged, dressed in an old dress, has a flamboyant dress lying on the stage, has a piece of sandwich in a pocket

3- MAN ONE - military-type uniform

4- MAN TWO - in a suit

5- MAN THREE - has a sack around his neck containing saline solution, plasters; enters sitting on the bottom shelf of a trolley

6- GIRL - has a bag/backpack filled with things including a mirror and ground cloth

Running Time

approx 60 mins

The events of this drama take place somewhere like nowhere but it can be anywhere, including a stall in the middle of a piazza, a house in a crowded street, a building in a park which is a public place of recreation, or a warehouse in a great overcrowded store.

On one side of the stage, there's a platform, 60 cm in height. It might be the pedestal of a sculpture or something ornamental. A few [as many as possible] doors are seen at the end of the stage. The stage darkens. Silence and darkness prevail for a few seconds. All of a sudden, a terrible explosion along with a glare shakes everywhere. Then again darkness and silence prevail and from the heart, different sirens, multiple explosions, car horns, hubbub, prolonged howls, loud laughs, various kinds of music, and any other possible sounds that introduce throng and chaos are heard with the passage of time. Then the stage lights up little by little and the sounds abate along with it till the stage lights up completely.

A YOUNG MAN is seen; dressed in filthy rags, sitting on the pedestal like the "The Thinker" sculpture by Auguste Rodin.

On the other side of the stage, a middle-aged WOMAN, dressed in a stained filthy court dress, is characteristically sitting downstage like the "Mona Lisa" portrait, that is with the same mysterious smile and penetrating look.

The sound of an approaching train whistle is heard. It seems that the train is crossing in front of the WOMAN's eyes and getting away.

Both actors stay still.

YOUNG MAN: I know … they all will die.

              The WOMAN *looks at the audience and has a smile on her face.*

YOUNG MAN: Why are you looking at them all the time?

WOMAN: If not … what else shall I do?

YOUNG MAN: [*pause*] I don't know … maybe … nothing.

WOMAN: Nothing again … Why are they here?

YOUNG MAN: I don't know … maybe … [*silence*]

WOMAN: Maybe what?

YOUNG MAN: I don't know … Ask them.

WOMAN: Can they hear us?

YOUNG MAN: I don't know … maybe … no.

WOMAN: Aha … [*still like the portrait of Mona Lisa*] Do you mean they are that far from us?!

YOUNG MAN: No …

WOMAN: So, they surely see us … don't they?

YOUNG MAN: I don't know … maybe they don't!

WOMAN: But we see them well, don't we?

YOUNG MAN: Uh-huh …

WOMAN: We can even see their sparkling eyes in darkness.

YOUNG MAN: They always sit in darkness and look at us.

WOMAN: But their looks are somehow strange … It scares me.

YOUNG MAN: Maybe because they see nothing.

WOMAN: How sad! … Do you mean they neither see nor hear us?

YOUNG MAN: I don't know … maybe.

WOMAN: So, they are like those who lived in caves in the past.

YOUNG MAN: In caves?!

WOMAN: Yeah … do you remember?

YOUNG MAN:	They all must have been killed ... but someone saved them.
WOMAN:	Who?
YOUNG MAN:	I don't know ... maybe ... but who was he? ... Yeah, there must be someone.
WOMAN:	Yeah ... I think there must have been someone too ... [thinks] Since when have we been here, then?
YOUNG MAN:	I don't know ... Maybe for centuries.
WOMAN:	Uh-hah ... [thinks] Well, when did I give birth to you?
YOUNG MAN:	I don't know ... maybe at the same time ... maybe some time sooner or later ...
WOMAN:	It's possible! ... I've forgotten it ... What do you mean by the same time?
YOUNG MAN:	I mean the same time you gave birth to me.
WOMAN:	That's as it was fated.
YOUNG MAN:	Accepting such a fate, we have to be in a lot of pain now.
WOMAN:	Till when?
YOUNG MAN:	I don't know ... Maybe forever.
WOMAN:	Forever! ... Till when does forever last?
YOUNG MAN:	[shouting] Oh ... You have no sense of time!
WOMAN:	Stop shouting at me ... Well, what shall I do? ... Because I kept staying here doing something repeatedly so much, I've forgotten everything.
YOUNG MAN:	I'm sorry ... I'm tired.
WOMAN:	It's too hard for me. Tolerating that you're tormented all the time ...
YOUNG MAN:	I know ... I wish you would go away from here.
WOMAN:	Go away?! ... Where?
YOUNG MAN:	Somewhere away from here ... Somewhere you'd be out of reach of everybody.

WOMAN:	I've never been to … Where is there?
YOUNG MAN:	I don't know … maybe … we'd better search and find it.
WOMAN:	No … I can't go … They'll kill you … Right … They'd kill you if I go … They said so themselves.
YOUNG MAN:	So, we have to tolerate such pain together every day.
WOMAN:	No … Let's run away together.
YOUNG MAN:	Where shall we go, if we run away?
WOMAN:	Somewhere far from here that you were talking about … We can find it, can't we?
YOUNG MAN:	I don't know … Maybe we can't find it anywhere.
WOMAN:	So, do we have to stay here forever?
YOUNG MAN:	I don't know … Maybe.
WOMAN:	We've been forgotten … We're walled up … Despite us removing the fourth wall, nobody sees us.
YOUNG MAN:	Well, it must be due to that sin I committed.
WOMAN:	I remember nothing … but I'd acquit you if I still were a judge.
YOUNG MAN:	What are you talking about?! … How can you acquit me when you even don't know what kind of sin I've committed?
WOMAN:	Well … I remember just a little of it … But I acquit you because you're my son.
YOUNG MAN:	Am I your son?!
WOMAN:	Yeah … You'd better not want to say you're not.
YOUNG MAN:	Say what is my name if I'm your son?
WOMAN:	At that time, your name …
YOUNG MAN:	What about now? What's my name right now?
WOMAN:	Your name … now?! … Aren't you hungry now?
YOUNG MAN:	Hungry! … You mean again …

WOMAN:	I've brought some food for you. [*takes two sand-wiches out of her pocket and holds out one of them to the* YOUNG MAN] Come on. Have it.
YOUNG MAN:	No … No, I'm not hungry.
WOMAN:	You are … Come on. Have it.
YOUNG MAN:	No … I'm not … I don't want to eat it.
WOMAN:	Do you want to stay hungry?
YOUNG MAN:	Yeah … Take it away.
WOMAN:	Well, you'll die then.
YOUNG MAN:	[*points at the sandwich*] I don't want it. I'll die even if I have it.
WOMAN:	No way out … We have just these … Take it.
YOUNG MAN:	[*gets the sandwich with hesitation and sniffs it*] It's too stale this time … It stinks.
WOMAN:	[*sniffs her own sandwich*] Same as always … It doesn't stink that much.
YOUNG MAN:	It's rotten … It's not safe to eat.
WOMAN:	Have it … [*begins eating and talks with her mouth full*] It's the only food we have …. We have nothing else to eat.
YOUNG MAN:	It's poisonous … Its smell makes me sick.
WOMAN:	Have it … or you'll stay hungry … You must have gotten used to it by now.
YOUNG MAN:	[*throws the morsel on the ground*] I won't eat it …
WOMAN:	[*goes hastily, picks up the morsel, removes the dust, and sniffs it. Then puts it in her pocket*] Well, it stinks a little but there's no way out … You don't know how I have to tolerate stinkier bodies to earn such food … [*with a lump in her throat*] Then you … Won't you have it for my sake … and throw it on the ground?
YOUNG MAN:	I can't help it … It makes me sick.
WOMAN:	No matter … I'll keep it for you …

YOUNG MAN: It's getting dark … They'll show up soon.

WOMAN: [*in haste*] I should get ready …

She takes a flamboyant and brassy dress out of a bin and tries it on but doesn't wear it.

YOUNG MAN: Who are they?

WOMAN: I don't know … They change day in, day out.

YOUNG MAN: Where do they take you?

WOMAN: I don't know … Wherever possible.

YOUNG MAN: Don't they bother you?

WOMAN: Bother?! … No … quite the contrary, they treat me very well and respect me.

YOUNG MAN: You're lying … I witnessed that myself …

WOMAN: Stop bothering yourself if you do nothing … So, never ask me who they are, where we go, and how they treat me.

YOUNG MAN: I should know about it … When that son of a bitch, I mean the dealer, makes anybody break the law, he indeed makes the justice …

WOMAN: [*begins laughing loudly and disgustingly*] Justice! …

YOUNG MAN: Stop laughing like that … It bothers me.

WOMAN: [*stops laughing and her face looks sad*] Ok … I don't laugh anymore … I couldn't help it … but you should stay alive … I have to stoop to do this job in order for you not to be killed. [*holds the dress out to herself*] Aside from this job, how could we show who we are?

YOUNG MAN: We're still in pain, therefore we are.

WOMAN: This dress comes more into sight … doesn't it?

YOUNG MAN: I hate this dress.

The YOUNG MAN squats down. In order not to see his mother, he bows his head, and holds it between his hands on his knees. The WOMAN goes toward him and holds his head in her hands.

WOMAN:	Don't worry, dear ... Look, this dress must be flamboyant to attract someone's attention.
YOUNG MAN:	But I like this one ... [points at the court dress his mother is wearing]
WOMAN:	It's too stained and filthy ... It's of no value anymore.
YOUNG MAN:	If I lose you, I'll be alone ... or may die.
WOMAN:	O'! ... Never do I leave you ... I won't let you die.
YOUNG MAN:	Tell me where my father is, if you really mean it.
WOMAN:	Your father?! ... Well, he's in heaven ...
YOUNG MAN:	No ... it's something written in the books ... Tell me where he is now.
WOMAN:	He! ... [pause]
YOUNG MAN:	Yeah, my father ... He's not in his own position ... Am I right?
WOMAN:	Poor guy ... His situation is worse than ours.
YOUNG MAN:	Did they kill him?
WOMAN:	No ... they castrated him.
YOUNG MAN:	Castrated?! ... My father?
WOMAN:	Yeah ... Then they dug a very deep hole and threw him in.
YOUNG MAN:	Well, say that he's dead and they buried him.
WOMAN:	No ... he's not dead. He's just lying in that hole.
YOUNG MAN:	Well, who is in my father's position up there?
WOMAN:	I don't know ... maybe nobody.
YOUNG MAN:	I know ... There must be someone ... Someone who is in my father's position ... Someone who is the most powerful among all.
WOMAN:	How do you know it?
YOUNG MAN:	[pause] I thought it so ... [pause] I feel hungry again.

WOMAN: [*takes the sandwich from her pocket and gives it to the* YOUNG MAN] There's no way out ... We've got nothing else.

YOUNG MAN: [*takes the sandwich and bites into it unwillingly, as if he's chewing gum and can't swallow the morsel*] It's so stinky it makes every bit of me bitter.

WOMAN: It's not more bitter than the bad breath of those you may see just once forever.

YOUNG MAN: No ... it's dirty ... [*spits up the morsel with disgust*] It's dirty! ... [*puts the sandwich in his pocket*] Till when shall we eat poisonous food? ... Right, we've got used to it because we've turned into poison too ... a deadly poison ... [*laughs*] A kind of poison that can kill all ... Yeah, we kill all people ...

Silence

YOUNG MAN: Say something ... I gibbered about it ... [*approaches the* WOMAN *and looks at her while standing in front of her*] Are you crying?

WOMAN: [*wipes her tears hastily*] Crying?! ... No ... a pesky mosquito is wandering around here these days which likes going into my eyes and jumping out ... [*startles*] O' gosh! ... My make-up ... I've not put on my make-up yet ... You'd better get up and take care of your appearance ... You're not to be untidy when they arrive ... Get up, good boy ... Get up.

YOUNG MAN: I've never thought that those who enlighten people will suffer such harsh and prolonged punishment.

WOMAN: [*sits on the pedestal and gets busy putting on make-up*] Well then ... One day, you told people what you shouldn't say ... So, stop nagging so much.

YOUNG MAN: None of them would have stayed alive if I didn't do that ... All would die.

WOMAN: You really messed everything up ... It's not ok that they see you like this ... Get up ... We should get ready.

YOUNG MAN: It's too difficult for us to be surrounded by so many people but not seen by them ... We're too lonely ... Desperately lonely, far from all ... [*looks around, then stares at the auditorium*] I think we have to re-move all the walls ... Everything looks better this way.

WOMAN: [*still busy putting on make-up*] Do you know what will happen then?! ... We can ...

The sound of a moving and whistling train resonates in a way that the WOMAN's *voice isn't heard anymore. We only see her lips moving. After a few seconds, the sound of the train gradually whooshes away and silence prevails for a while. The* YOUNG MAN *takes a few steps following the train, then stops and looks at the railway track lying ahead. (It could be that the* YOUNG MAN – *who is following the moving train – looks and turns his head downstage as if the railway passes through the audience or they are all on board the train.)*

YOUNG MAN: All will die ...!

WOMAN: I have a strange feeling.

YOUNG MAN: [*dealing with his inner conflicts*] No ... Impossible!

WOMAN: Why ... do I experience such a kind of feeling when-ever I put on make-up?

YOUNG MAN: [*still dealing with his inner conflicts*] So strange!

WOMAN: It's quite usual ... I always ask myself if they like me this time too.

YOUNG MAN: Is it possible?!

WOMAN: There's no way out ... It turns into something common after a while.

YOUNG MAN: No ... this path leads to destruction.

WOMAN: [*finishes putting on make-up*] What did you say?

YOUNG MAN: I'm talking about this railway ...

WOMAN:	Which one? ... [*draws a line in the air with her finger downstage indicating the railway*] Do you mean the same railway the train already passed through?
YOUNG MAN:	Yeah ... How come? Is there any other railway around here?
WOMAN:	[*looks around*] No ...
YOUNG MAN:	Seems you begin to lose your memory day by day ... I'm afraid that one day you'll lose your way coming here too.
WOMAN:	No ... I'll never lose you.
YOUNG MAN:	Why not ...? One day in the evening you'll leave me and never return.
WOMAN:	No ... I'll return.
YOUNG MAN:	So, keep this railroad in mind if you don't want to lose your way here.
WOMAN:	[*looks at the both sides of the railway*] Ok ... Where does it lead to then?
YOUNG MAN:	Nowhere.
WOMAN:	Nowhere isn't a place ... The train made a lot of noise.
YOUNG MAN:	Yeah ... It just made a lot of noise ... but the rail has broken a little farther ahead, before the next town.
WOMAN:	Oh gosh! ... How horrible! ... Well, where did it go at speed?
YOUNG MAN:	To the bottom of a valley ... a very deep one that leads to darkness.
WOMAN:	How bad! ... Do you mean with all on board?!
YOUNG MAN:	Right ... with all on board ...
WOMAN:	What will happen to them now?
	Silence
WOMAN:	They may die ... That's right, I know ... They'll surely die ... O'! ... They must have been terrified ... Don't you think?

YOUNG MAN: Maybe ... But no, they haven't been terrified.

WOMAN: Haven't been terrified?! ... Impossible ... Imagine that ...

YOUNG MAN: They don't know ... They don't know where they're going.

WOMAN: [*wants to go hastily*] Well, we should let them know about it.

YOUNG MAN: In order for them to be horrified?

WOMAN: But we should do something, shouldn't we?

YOUNG MAN: No ... It doesn't help them anymore.

WOMAN: Poor guys ...!

YOUNG MAN: It's heading downhill and can't be stopped.

WOMAN: How awful! ... So much the better, they don't know about it ... They are at ease of mind this way.

YOUNG MAN: Maybe ... By the way, its brakes might have failed.

WOMAN: Even worse ... Did you see the driver?

YOUNG MAN: Driver?! Was there any?

WOMAN: I don't know ... It was running at full speed. I could see nothing.

YOUNG MAN: I didn't either.

WOMAN: Maybe there was a driver but he felt sleepy and went to sleep along with the passengers.

YOUNG MAN: Maybe ... The rail has been broken anyway.

WOMAN: Then the train is heading out on its own and they don't know where they're going ... But they'll finally have to know about it, won't they?

             Silence. The YOUNG MAN *is still looking at the rail-way on which the train passed.*

WOMAN: But what's the use of it?! ... All of them will die then ... Yeah, they'll die ... Do you think they first become aware of it and then die ... or they first die and then become aware of it?

YOUNG MAN: I don't know … Maybe it wouldn't matter anymore.

WOMAN: Yeah, you're right … It doesn't matter to them anymore … Poor guys! … I should get changed … they'll show up soon.

The WOMAN *picks up her flamboyant dress and exits through a door. The* YOUNG MAN *takes the sandwich out of his pocket and lifts it to his mouth, but feels sick. A knock at the door is heard. He hides the sandwich in a corner hurriedly. Then goes toward one of the doors and opens it. But no one is there. The sound of laughter is heard. The* YOUNG MAN *opens another door. Again, there's no one at the door. Sounds of laughter and slamming of another door are heard.*

YOUNG MAN: Let me say that you're at this door … [*opens another door. Nobody is there. The sound of laughter is heard again.*] Oh … where are you then?

The doors slam one after another and along with them the sound of a few people is heard who are laughing loudly. Each time the YOUNG MAN *goes hastily to open one of the doors but he can't open it and runs towards another door as he hears the sound of laughter and slam of another door. But he is deceived again and runs between the doors confusedly. He finally stops before one of the doors, tired and burned out. He goes toward one of the doors with the intention of surprising someone and opens it suddenly. Nobody is there. A loud guffaw is heard and another door opens following it.* TWO MEN *enter the stage hurriedly. They are wearing formal and chic clothes but they both look ridiculous and caricature-like due to the color and shape of the clothes.*

MAN ONE: Aww, how funny! … You've been double-crossed again, haven't you?

YOUNG MAN:	You're cheating … You enter from a different door each time.
MAN TWO:	We arrived on time.
MAN ONE:	Say it now … Hurry up … say that we double-crossed you again this time.
MAN TWO:	As usual.
YOUNG MAN:	With all these doors that you made …
MAN ONE:	Uh … you weren't supposed to cheat.
MAN TWO:	I'm ready …
MAN ONE:	Confess that we've double-crossed you.
MAN TWO:	We should start … Confess!
YOUNG MAN:	Confess to what?
MAN ONE:	Confess that we cheated you … I mean you've been deceived.
YOUNG MAN:	Anybody would be deceived this way too.
MAN TWO:	I'm ready … Shall we start?
MAN ONE:	Well, did you confess? … Do you admit that we're more cunning than you?
MAN TWO:	He did.
YOUNG MAN:	Ok … Leave me alone, you crazies. I did confess … Are you now at ease of mind?
MAN ONE:	Yeah, how funny it is.
YOUNG MAN:	Is it your turn this time?
MAN ONE:	You see what it is …
MAN TWO:	I'm ready. Shall we start?
YOUNG MAN:	Where's your noble dealer then?
MAN ONE:	Gee … what do you do with him? … We top anybody else.
MAN TWO:	The master told us to get started. He'll come later.
	The WOMAN *in her flamboyant dress and with heavy make-up – heavier than in the previous scene*

	– enters the stage pushing a trolley with plenty of food. A white cloth covers the trolley down to its wheels. The men look passionately at the WOMAN coming in.
MAN ONE:	Aww ... how beautiful and brilliant!
MAN TWO:	It's the taste that counts.
MAN ONE:	But her beauty and appearance matter most to me.
MAN TWO:	But to me, the taste matters most ... I mean it's the taste that counts.
MAN ONE:	Nope, you should first pay attention to her beauty and elegance.
MAN TWO:	I don't care a fig about appearance ... when it's going to be eaten, no matter how beautiful it is.
MAN ONE:	Damn you! You really lack any sense of aesthetics.
MAN TWO:	What did you say that I lack?
MAN ONE:	Feeling ... I mean emotion.
MAN TWO:	I don't lack it ... Who said so?
MAN ONE:	You're all wet ... You wouldn't be that impassive if you had any sense of it.
MAN TWO:	Really? ... I'll show you.
	MAN TWO *rushes to the trolley but* MAN ONE *stops him.*
MAN ONE:	Wait ... You don't understand how much the beauty of the food setting can whet our appetite.
MAN TWO:	I don't understand what you're talking about ... [*pushes* MAN ONE *and rushes to the trolley*] I should have it out.
MAN THREE:	[*his voice is heard*] Stop it. Shut up ... Dear sirs, help yourself as you wish ... just shut your mouth.
	The WOMAN *keeps moving here and there to prepare the dinner table. She goes out, comes in, and does the table setting. She brings in some stools and whatever is needed from off stage. She moves*

so fast that she makes her last movement as the
FIRST TWO MEN *go to have dinner.*

MAN TWO: I'm ready, shall we start?

MAN ONE: Where's he himself then?

YOUNG MAN: As usual, his howling is heard first … Then he'll show up out of the blue.

MAN ONE: You must know why.

YOUNG MAN: Yeah … because they're crazy … there's something wrong with them.

MAN ONE: No dear, you're wrong … You should know that the speech and actions of prominent figures are always unpredictable.

YOUNG MAN: That's it … He'll enter in a civilized way if he isn't as crooked as a dog's hind leg.

MAN THREE: [*his voice is heard*] Aha … now who can say where I am?

Like children, MAN ONE *and* MAN TWO *nose around, behind the doors, among the audience, and … Then they return desperately.*

MAN ONE: Are you sure it was his own voice?

MAN TWO: Yeah … It was his own voice.

MAN ONE: Where's he himself then?

The sound of the MAN THREE's *laughter is heard.*

MAN TWO: You heard it, didn't you? … He's laughing.

MAN ONE: How unscrupulous and lovely he is! … He used to be the same as a child.

MAN TWO: He was like a ball of fire.

MAN ONE: No … he wasn't fire in nature … He played with fire … but once someone came and robbed him of it.

The sound of MAN THREE *is heard crying fraudulently.*

MAN ONE: O'… damn you who reminded him again.

MAN TWO:	You started first.
MAN ONE:	What difference does it make? … We've broken his heart.
MAN TWO:	I'm ready … Shall we start?
	MAN ONE *shakes his head. They coordinate with each other to go and take the white cloth away from the trolley.* MAN THREE, *an oddly-shaped man wearing tacky clothes, is sitting on the trolley's under-shelf. As the tablecloth is taken away, he jumps out, bounces up and down, and jubilates. A sack is slung around his neck.*
MAN THREE:	There now! … What did I tell you? You, the crazy, couldn't find me.
MAN TWO:	Ah! … I thought it was just a kind of game.
MAN ONE:	Shut up, you stupid!
MAN TWO:	Well, did I really screw up again?
MAN THREE:	You always screw up.
MAN TWO:	Well, I'm ready … Shall we start now?
MAN THREE:	[*turns to the* YOUNG MAN *and stays still for a second*] You again?! … [*attacks him*] I cornered you again … You're the same thief who robbed me of all my stuff.
MAN TWO:	Well, shall we start now?
MAN THREE:	[*to the* YOUNG MAN] Yeah … I well remember how you cheated me like the Devil, stole the fruits of my father's garden, and gave them to those poor guys.
YOUNG MAN:	Did you expect me to let that dotard kill all?
MAN ONE:	[*reacts in a way showing that he's surprised at what the* YOUNG MAN *said*] O' gosh! … [*to* MAN TWO] He said dotard.
MAN TWO:	What does it mean? … Shall we start now?

MAN THREE:	No, you stupid … [*to the* YOUNG MAN] Does it mean that you didn't know it was forbidden for them to eat those fruits?
YOUNG MAN:	No, swear to your father …
MAN THREE:	[*interrupts the* YOUNG MAN] Stop insulting my kind father … Don't call him a stupid rascal.
MAN ONE:	No … I know he wanted to call him dotard.
MAN TWO:	[*to* MAN THREE] It's you who calls your father rascal, sir.
MAN THREE:	I know it myself, you stupid … [*to the* YOUNG MAN] I know you've already disgraced that kind old man and made everybody disrespect him.
MAN TWO:	Shall we start now?
MAN THREE:	Now … now you must confess … that you are the same Sacred Devil … I give you enough time to confess … Hurry up! Come on … Confess it.
YOUNG MAN:	Stop it … You talked my head off. What shall I confess to?
MAN THREE:	Say that you're a thief … Say … [*turns to* MAN ONE *and* MAN TWO] why are you looking at me like a cat on hot bricks? …
MAN TWO:	Well, we can start …
MAN ONE:	O'! … Great!
	MAN ONE *and* MAN TWO *go toward the* WOMAN *and stand at the trolley so that they can keep an eye on* MAN THREE *while being entertained by the* WOMAN.
MAN THREE:	[*beckons to the* YOUNG MAN *to go to the other side of the stage*] You, the stupid rascal!
YOUNG MAN:	[*stops*] What?! … Talking to me?
MAN THREE:	Who else can I talk to? … Let's carry out the related law.

They go to the other side of the stage where they can be seen in full light. MAN THREE first gags and binds the YOUNG MAN, then takes the end of a white wide band out of a sack. The YOUNG MAN stays between bearing walls of two doors and MAN THREE bandages him up to present a combination of a mummy, scarecrow, and crucified man. This should be carried out in the time during which the THREE MEN finish the lines that are to be spoken.

MAN THREE: You know yourself … that I like you from the bottom of my heart … and I don't really want to do so.

MAN ONE & TWO: [*together*] We don't either … [*laugh loudly*]

MAN THREE: But I have to … You are fair and understand my situation … I have to torment you unwillingly in the worst way.

MAN TWO: Bind him tightly to death.

MAN THREE: I know well what to do … [*murmurs*] Rascal!

MAN ONE: Well … why do you hesitate? … Go ahead …

MAN THREE: Ok … [*to the* YOUNG MAN] Indeed, I myself suffer from tormenting you.

MAN ONE: Whew! … [*to* MAN TWO] What did he say?

MAN TWO: No matter … [*to* MAN THREE] Bind him tightly to death.

MAN THREE: How come I can torment my best friend?! … A friend who has done me the greatest service.

MAN ONE: O'! … [*to* MAN TWO] I didn't understand. What did he say?

MAN TWO: [*gets up, goes to the* YOUNG MAN, *and kicks him roughly on the leg*] Stand upright.

The YOUNG MAN *is writhing in pain.*

MAN THREE: Would you please let us be alone?

MAN TWO: Well, bind him tightly to death.

MAN THREE: Rascal … How dare you kick my friend!

MAN TWO:	It was the right time for it.
MAN THREE:	I know … I wanted to hit him myself.

MAN TWO *returns to his place.*

MAN THREE:	[*to the* YOUNG MAN] I'm sure you've already got it … But no, you've not yet understood that you robbed me of a fatal thing … You didn't know the other qualifications of fire rather than heat and light … Ouch! … It's started again … [*begins scratching his body with avidity in a way that he loses control of himself*] You rascals, why are you just sitting there? … Come and help me.
MAN TWO:	We should scratch his body.
MAN ONE:	Aww … how exciting!

MAN ONE *and* MAN TWO *begin whirling around and sometimes scratch his body while clapping and exulting.* MAN THREE *twists, jumps up and down, rolls around, and moans out of pain and joy along with frenetic laughter. It seems that an animal instinct has arisen in him. After finishing with his work, he gets up and tidies himself.*

MAN THREE:	[*to the other two*] Thanks, sirs … Follow through with your job.
MAN ONE:	Aww … what pleasure we had!
MAN TWO:	Let's follow through with our job.

MAN ONE *and* MAN TWO *go to the* WOMAN. MAN THREE *goes to the* YOUNG MAN.

MAN THREE:	Here is my share of the patrimony! … My father owns plenty of land, estate, cattle and sheep but I've inherited the itching from him instead … You know, this kind of rash is an inheritance I've received from my family … I have to scratch the rash till it begins breeding.
MAN TWO:	Bind him tightly to death.

MAN THREE:	[*To the* YOUNG MAN] Then I feel relief ... a painful pleasure ... Yeah, I know it was too painful for you when you found out how difficult it is to control the fire, and the flames which can turn anything into ash ... Yeah, I knew ... what disaster could happen if anybody accessed the fire ... In fact, I'd been informed that you wanted to steal it from me.
MAN ONE:	Well, we did it for you.
MAN THREE:	... What a good time it was ... [*to the* YOUNG MAN] When I first noticed, you made me so mad that I'd have ordered to cut you up ... but when I gave it some thought, I noticed you wanted to serve me well ... [*wraps the band so tightly around the* YOUNG MAN'*s neck that he reacts to the sharp pain*] Oh ... excuse me. I didn't hurt you, did I? ... Yeah, I noticed that my father wanted to kill all those poor guys and train some other people instead ... who obey him ...
	MAN TWO *steps forward and stands behind* MAN THREE *without him noticing.*
MAN THREE:	I said it led to my destruction ... You don't know how sneaky he is! ... He gets so caught up in such situations but he plays dumb in a way that all think he really knows nothing. But my dastardly father keeps an eye on everything ... Quite the contrary, when he puts on a straight face, he's sillier than ever ... [*scratches his body for a while*]
MAN TWO:	Shall I scratch it for you?
MAN THREE:	What are you doing here?
MAN TWO:	I'm listening to you ... but set your mind at ease and say what you wish ... I'm behind you all the way.
MAN THREE:	[*points at where the* WOMAN *is standing*] Go there and do your job.
MAN TWO:	Your father asked me to watch over you and see if you bind him tightly to death.

MAN THREE: Anyway, he knows that I want to do something against him …

MAN TWO: Well, go ahead … because he himself had played hell with his father before. I remember it well … To became a king, you must kill the king first.

MAN THREE: [*tidies up the* YOUNG MAN'*s hair*] Yeah … I, like him, know what to do.

MAN TWO: You let him [*points at the* YOUNG MAN] help you too. [*laughs loudly*]

MAN THREE: [*laughs*] Shut up, you the rascal … Now all think [*to the* YOUNG MAN] that you made them aware on your own. You said that my father is to kill them all … but nobody knows that I myself … the main information …

MAN TWO: We ourselves …

MAN THREE: Right … we provided you with them … and you, like a devoted warrior, could save all people from the fate awaiting them … [*bows down before the* YOUNG MAN] You are really a great man … who risked his life to save humanity and now has to experience death one thousand times a day.

MAN TWO: [*kicks the* YOUNG MAN *in the leg so brutally that he loses his balance*] Do you have ants in your pants? … Stand upright and let him pay homage to you …

MAN THREE: I have to do these things anyway … [*wraps the band tightly around the* YOUNG MAN'*s body*]

MAN TWO: It's an order from your father … It should be thoroughly obeyed …

MAN THREE: You two …

MAN TWO: I know … Do you want to say that we are such nouveau riche bastards who spy for your father? … Bind it much more tightly.

MAN THREE: But you should know that you are the best clients of mine.

MAN TWO:	[*looks at MAN ONE*] You should act normal in order for him not to notice that you are allies ... Bind him tightly to death.
	The YOUNG MAN *tries to say something but fails.* MAN THREE *is still busy binding him.*
MAN THREE:	Ok ... but my father has now turned to be a real dotard ... He, of course, has been stupid from the very beginning but not old. He got old later.
MAN TWO:	As you said, he's now turned to become a bastard too.
MAN THREE:	[*laughs and turns to the* YOUNG MAN *while binding him*] Well, we together could give him what for ... [*kisses the* YOUNG MAN] I get excited whenever I remember it ... What if not for you?! [*all of a sudden, abandons his work and begins scratching his body severely*] Help ... Come and scratch my body ...
MAN ONE:	Ooh ... shall we keep scratching?
	MAN ONE *and* MAN TWO *begin exulting and whirling around* MAN THREE *while scratching his body. On the brink of insanity,* MAN THREE *keeps scratching his body and rolling around while moaning in pain and pleasure. He falls, worn-out.*
MAN ONE:	Leave him alone ... It's over.
MAN TWO:	We scratched his father's body for a lifetime and now it's his turn ... I got sick and tired ...
MAN ONE:	Ooh! ... Sounds great.
MAN TWO:	That sounds great to you, not me.
MAN ONE:	That's great to you too, idiot.
MAN TWO:	How come?
MAN ONE:	What the hell are you asking about? ... How difficult you are to work with.
MAN TWO:	I'm not so difficult, am I?

MAN ONE:	How shall I know? ... I've got nothing to do with you anymore.
MAN TWO:	But I have.
MAN THREE:	[*gets up with difficulty*] Shut up ... Stop talking non-sense! ...
MAN ONE:	He meant you.
MAN TWO:	What are you talking about? ... How come?
MAN THREE:	[*still feels listless*] You haven't finished with your work, have you?
MAN ONE:	No ... in fact ... In fact, what? [*to* MAN TWO]
MAN TWO:	Shall we start?
MAN ONE:	No need to start ... Let's continue.
MAN TWO:	You've always ditched me ... I still ...
MAN THREE:	[*shouting*] Go and do what the hell you wish ... Just go away.

Both of them go to the WOMAN. MAN THREE *stands before the* YOUNG MAN.

MAN THREE: He's so awkward ... [*points at* MAN ONE *and* MAN TWO] I don't mean them who are rouges. I mean my father who still thinks he should kill anybody whom he doesn't like one way or the other ... [*while wrapping the bandage around the* YOUNG MAN] but I, like you, disagree with it ... You, of course, made a big mistake ... You thought people could find their way if they had a quest for knowledge ... But no, it's not right, good boy ... Do you know why?... Aha, cling to the wall more tightly ... You don't need to say anything ... because you've not experienced any cruises ... I own a great ship of my own and I've never left the rudder to anybody else to steer ... Stop moving around ... You see! ... My mind is at ease if I take over the rudder myself. This way, no matter what others do in the ship, I can entertain them all ... then ask them to do as they wish ... They all are free to cry, laugh, and play hell with each other ... I even let them oppose and curse me but I'm the only helmsman ... Yeah, they all are free ... Stand upright and let me finish with you ... No matter if all people in my ship are criminal, virtuous, or even true-blue revolutionaries ... [*stops working and begins scratching his body*]

MAN ONE: May I scratch your body?

MAN THREE: [*stops scratching*] No, it's over quickly this time.

MAN TWO: Well, bind him tightly to death.

MAN ONE: Aww! ... What a pleasure!

MAN THREE: [*points at* MAN ONE *and* MAN TWO *and quietly to the* YOUNG MAN] I hate their guts. They have voracious appetites because they've got nothing else to do ... Now they are among the prominent big shots of town ... but they are so stingy and cheap-skate despite owning a great amount of wealth ... They didn't give me much money for tonight but last night's clients were such generous idiots ... They gave me a great deal of money ... You see, we'll make a fortune if I come across such clients every night ... This way, we can at least earn the money needed for their dinner and entertainment ...

MAN TWO: It's your turn ...

MAN ONE: Why? I'll get tired.

MAN TWO: Go ahead ...

MAN ONE: Damn you, idiot ... [*approaches* MAN THREE] Well, we are in need of something anyway ... Who else would meet our needs but you? ... You, of course, said what you wanted to say. You have some demands to be met instead ...

MAN THREE: We fail to live otherwise ... [*murmurs*] Nouveau riche bastards!

MAN ONE: We'll let your father know there's something between you two ...

MAN THREE:	What do you mean? ... You bastard spies.
MAN ONE:	Ooh! ... Why are you cursing?
MAN THREE:	You should be happy that I give you my father's title ... [*to the* YOUNG MAN] You see they are too unreliable ... Do you know how they earned all their money tonight?
MAN ONE:	Well, we're into keeping count of our earnings ... from your father ...
MAN THREE:	Yeah, you've got it from my bastard father ... [shouting] as your reward for spying on me.
MAN ONE:	Ooh! ... Don't shout at me.
MAN THREE:	I do ... Do you know why? ... Because you have all the fun and pleasures for free.
MAN ONE:	You're nasty ... I'm going to leave here. You'll say that I'm an idiot too ... [*goes in a different direction and sits alone*]
MAN THREE:	Right, you are as idiotic as my father ... [*to the* YOUNG MAN] They think I'm an idiot of course ... They think that my father is an idiot ... By the way, my father thinks the same about them ... In fact, eveybody thinks that the other is an idiot.
MAN ONE:	Sounds good! ... We've got along with each other this way ... Will you begin quarreling with me if I step forward?
MAN THREE:	Yeah, I'll beat you too ... [*to the* YOUNG MAN *in a way that they can't hear. But it seems that they hear him because they've perked up their ears and* MAN ONE *reacts accordingly*] They don't know I'm snatching my father's wealth and power this way ... They are helping me too ... and enjoy themselves as well in the meantime. It serves them right ... Look at them carefully ... They know nothing but enjoyment ... Well, they are right. These all are my father's faults ... He doubts everybody due to his own weak-ness and misery ... Nobody knows ... All may think

my father is ruler of the world but I know how nasty he is.

MAN ONE: Did you call us?

MAN TWO: Bind him tightly to death.

MAN THREE: Keep on enjoying as much as possible right now … [*angrily*] Yeah, Enjoy yourselves rascals … [*to the* YOUNG MAN] Did you hear? … I told them to keep on enjoying … Yeah, he's one of those miserable henpecked men.

MAN ONE: Ooh! … Do you mean that I'm miserable?

MAN THREE: Did you mishear me again? … I'm talking about my father who always wants to vent his anger on people around.

MAN ONE: O', I know … but nobody knows that he bullies them into doing something out of weakness not strength.

MAN THREE: You know better … He, the rascal, knows well how to play his role.

MAN ONE: Ooh, I wish I was dead … [*goes to the* YOUNG MAN *and touches his chest*] You didn't take care of yourself again … What's this injury on your chest for? … [*to* MAN THREE] Please bandage up his wound … No, I should clean it with saline solution first … Oh! … [*takes a bottle of saline solution and medical plaster out of the sack slung around* MAN THREE*'s neck*] It may get infected. [*opens the bottle and pours the solution on his chest*] Our mind is at ease this way.

              The YOUNG MAN *is writhing in pain and wants to shout.*

MAN THREE: That's ok now. I should wrap it up. [*sets about wrapping the bandage around the wound*]

MAN TWO: Bind him tightly to death.

MAN ONE: By doing so, you make your father trust you.

MAN THREE: I told you to think about the money you've paid in advance for tonight … Go and enjoy yourself.

MAN ONE: [*turns to* MAN TWO *and the* WOMAN *while leaving*] Shake a leg, get it done … I can't stand it anymore.

MAN THREE: Don't you want me to make my father trust me more? … [*to the* YOUNG MAN] At long last, I'll be forced to kill him … as he killed my grandpa too … Yeah, right … I have to get the hell out of my rascal father in order not to break with this lasting tradition of our family.

MAN ONE: Ooh … Why do you keep on talking about your father?

MAN THREE: Just to remember him. That's it … Right, we should respect the traditions … [*pauses for a while and then begins scratching his body severely while moving more earnestly than before. Beside saying nonsense, snoring, and drawing long breath, he is frothing at the mouth. He finally crumples to the floor and bursts into shrieks of hysterical laugher. Neither of the other two come to help him*] Damn my father and this family inheritance … [*to the* YOUNG MAN] Don't worry. I'll come back. Your number is up … [*points at the other two*] They have enough time to help and enjoy themselves too … [*pauses for a while. Then the men burst into shrieks of laughter.* MAN THREE *gets up self-confidently but languidly and tidies himself*] But I'll do it in my own way …

    The sound of an approaching train whistle is heard, then resonates throughout, and slowly goes away.

MAN THREE: [*to the* YOUNG MAN] Does it sound familiar to you? … Huh! … I guess you've forgotten it … but I'll remind you now … You were the first who helped the idea cross people's minds to make it … Now I own it … There was no way out to take my father down a peg. Poor guy would like me to hold onto his lands, cattle and sheep like himself but he didn't know that I'm a bastard like himself ... [*gets busy wrapping the bandage around the* YOUNG MAN's *head and face*] It's over ... To gain more power than him, I had to make the train speed up day by day in a way that it became unknown even for you who had planned to build it ... [*wraps the bandage around the* YOUNG MAN's *head and face.*] It works better this way.

MAN ONE: Finished?

MAN THREE: Yes ... finished ... [*murmurs*] Wait your turn.

MAN TWO: Did you bind him tightly to death?

MAN THREE: [*moves a few steps from the* YOUNG MAN *who is now bandaged all over and looks carefully at him like a painter or sculptor who examines at his own work*] No ... It expresses no feeling ... [*goes forward, takes a few brushes and some paint out of the sack, and begins painting something on his face. In the end, the portrait of a laughing clown is seen*] You know well how much I like you ... So, smile ... I'd like your face to be happy and lovely ... Smile, you the Sacred Devil ... Smile because you've attracted the attention of all by keeping silent ... Smile ...

MAN ONE *and* MAN TWO *burst into laughter. Then they sit the* WOMAN *on the trolley's upper surface, whirl around the stage while singing out of happiness, and approach* MAN THREE. *Like a sculpture, the* WOMAN *looks cold and has bowed her head while tilted to the side.*

MAN ONE: [*stands briefly before the* YOUNG MAN] Aww, what a wonderful piece of work! ... I congratulate you ... [*shakes* MAN THREE's *hand*] Believe me, I really admire your work of art ... Your father would surely admire it.

MAN TWO: [*looks carefully at the* YOUNG MAN *and assures himself that the* YOUNG MAN *has been tightly*

	bound] You've bound him well … I'll let the master know you've bound him tightly to death.
MAN THREE:	Yes … look at his smile …
MAN ONE:	This sculpture is a masterpiece, dear … masterpiece!
MAN THREE:	I told you to look at his smile, you the bastard!
MAN ONE:	Yes … it's a masterpiece … as if he's kept on smiling for centuries.
MAN THREE:	Isn't it worth being maintained forever?
MAN ONE:	Anyway … we can hang it from somewhere with a rope for everybody to watch it.
MAN TWO:	So what?
MAN ONE:	In order for all to see how a happy and smiling face can make others happy … so enjoyable … I wish you could paint his lips in bold red … Dash it all! …
	MAN THREE *paints the* YOUNG MAN's *lips in bold red with a brush and some paint. The* WOMAN *looks gently at the* YOUNG MAN, *then at the audience, and bows her head again as if a very heavy load is slung around her neck.*
MAN THREE:	Let's go … He stays here in order for all to see that everybody is happy in this town.
MAN TWO:	… to death.
MAN ONE:	Yes, let's go … [*to* MAN THREE] After you …
	MAN THREE *sits on the trolley's lower surface and they all leave the stage singing together. The* YOUNG MAN *stays for a few seconds as if he smiles at the audience. A young* GIRL *wearing a backpack enters the stage. She enters wanting to assure herself whether anybody is on the stage. She stops as she sees the* YOUNG MAN *and shows her respect to him.*
GIRL:	Hi … [*goes a bit closer*] I said hello … Oh! … [*steps back a bit out of horror*] I … I'm sorry … Well, what shall I do? … I'm afraid … [*cowers in a way that*

seems she feels cold] You've got nothing to do with me ... have you? [*goes forward again with fear and caution. Seeing him closely this time puts her in a kind of different mood*] Aww, how funny you are! ... [*bursts into laughter*] Aww, what a lovely scare-crow! ... [*goes forward and touches the* YOUNG MAN. *All the paints get mingled as she touches his face. The* GIRL *fears and steps back a bit*] You ... What are you?

The YOUNG MAN *moves gently.*

GIRL: Aww, how nice ... You're a human! ... [*goes forward and looks at him again*] Why have they bound you if you're a human? ... Would you like me to unbind you? ... You must like it but what a pity that you can't talk. Otherwise you would say that you'd like to get free ... [*gets busy unbinding him. First, she un-binds the bandage from his face and the* YOUNG MAN's *face appears. The* GIRL *startles happily*] Hi ... Aww, how nice! ... You are a real human ... [*while the* GIRL *unbinds the bandage off the* YOUNG MAN's *hands and legs, she keeps talking with him, quite contrary to the way* MAN THREE *was talking with him while binding him up*] Do you know ...? At first, when I saw you from a distance, I thought you'd been crucified ... I really felt pity on you ... but when I came closer, I thought you were a mummy. To be honest, it really scared me but I was so tired that I thought no need to fear. To have a mummy as a companion is much better than being left alone and vagrant ... That's why I came closer ... but you won't believe it if I say that you looked like a very funny scarecrow when I came a bit closer and saw your painted face ... [*laughs*] I was so happy that you weren't a mummy to scare me ... I said to myself how nice it is! ... I've now found a kind scarecrow which I can stay and talk with forever ... Ooh, how tightly they've bound it around your neck! ... How nice that you've not been stifled ... I don't want you to die ... Aww, how nice that you're an alive human! ... [*tries hard to untie one of the knots*] What a square knot it is! ... It's hard to be untied ...

The YOUNG MAN *makes her understand to open his mouth by giving her a wink, moving his head, and moaning. The* GIRL *takes the cloth off his mouth.*

YOUNG MAN: Who are you? ...

GIRL: [*still unbinding him*] Me?! ... You say who you are.

YOUNG MAN: You see ... I've got stuck here ... Untie my hands first.

GIRL: [*unties the* YOUNG MAN*'s hands.*] Ooh! ... Who has bound you this way?

YOUNG MAN: [*Unwraps the bandage from his body*] I didn't think anybody could see us anymore! ... Where have you come from?

GIRL: I'm ... from anywhere you can think ... I've traveled all around.

YOUNG MAN: [*takes the sandwich out of his pocket to eat*] Aah ... how stinky!

GIRL: No, don't have it ... I've brought you some food.

YOUNG MAN: I'm starving.

GIRL: [*gets the sandwich from the* YOUNG MAN *and sniffs it*] Aah ... it's poisonous ... [*puts her backpack on the floor and begins looking for something in it*]

YOUNG MAN: How did you understand it?

GIRL: Because it's foul-smelling.

YOUNG MAN: I know it myself.

GIRL: Great! ... Well, why did you want to have it then?

YOUNG MAN: I said that I was starving ... I asked you how you understood that I was starving?

GIRL: Well, everybody who feels hungry, eats something.

YOUNG MAN: Yeah ... You're right ... I was eating food.

GIRL:	Un-huh … [*takes a sandwich out of her backpack and gives it to the* YOUNG MAN] Come on … Have it … I cooked it myself.
YOUNG MAN:	[*takes and sniffs the sandwich*] Smells delicious!
GIRL:	It tastes delicious too … I cooked it myself.
YOUNG MAN:	Yeah … I know.
GIRL:	Great! … Well, do you know that I cooked it for you?
YOUNG MAN:	For me?! … Why?
GIRL:	Well, because you're hungry …
YOUNG MAN:	Aha … How did you know that we were here?
GIRL:	I saw you from a distance … but when I came closer and noticed that you were not a human, I got the blues.
YOUNG MAN:	What? … Did you say that I wasn't a human?!
GIRL:	I've already said it … First, I thought you'd been crucified … Then as I came closer, I thought that …
YOUNG MAN:	Yeah … that I'm a mummy … Once you said it.
GIRL:	But your mouth was gagged and couldn't answer …
YOUNG MAN:	[*pestered*] Look! … I really like your cooking …. Will you let me have it easy now?
GIRL:	Ok … Have it. I cooked it myself.
YOUNG MAN:	I'm sorry … [*bites into the sandwich*] How good and delicious it is!
GIRL:	I myself …
YOUNG MAN:	I know … You cooked it yourself.
GIRL:	Right … Do you love me now?
YOUNG MAN:	Aha … how delicious!
GIRL:	Sounds great! … [*takes a ground cloth out of her backpack and spreads it on the ground*] I can cook something for you again if you wish … [*takes some other stuff out of her backpack and puts it around*] As you wish.

YOUNG MAN:	[*notices the* GIRL] Hay, what are you doing?
GIRL:	I'm too tired ... [*lies down on the ground*] I found nowhere to take a rest.
YOUNG MAN:	Well ... you can rest till they arrive.
GIRL:	I've never stayed in a fixed place ... as far as I can remember ...
YOUNG MAN:	You didn't tell me your name.
GIRL:	Now ... what do you want to do with my name?
YOUNG MAN:	To know how to call you ... You look familiar to me.
GIRL:	Sounds great! ... Well, you know me, don't you?!
YOUNG MAN:	I guess so ... Will you finally tell me your name?
GIRL:	No ... I can't ... because I've been always homeless and a wanderer ... I've never talked with anybody so far ... I mean nobody dared to talk to me ... I always had to keep avoiding anyone who was following me like a gadfly ... I've forgotten everything... [*while saying these words, gets up and lays all the stuff on the floor tastefully*] ... even my own name ...
YOUNG MAN:	Excellent!
GIRL:	Is it because I've forgotten my own name?
YOUNG MAN:	No ... I mean the meal.
GIRL:	Does it taste delicious?
YOUNG MAN:	Yeah ...
GIRL:	Have it ... I cooked it myself.
YOUNG MAN:	Aha ... I know.
GIRL:	Well, tell me your name if you liked it.
YOUNG MAN:	After you ...
GIRL:	No ... after you ... You said that you knew me, didn't you?
YOUNG MAN:	Shall I say?
GIRL:	Aha ...

YOUNG MAN: Which name shall I say?!

GIRL: A good name ... A name which belongs to you.

YOUNG MAN: I don't remember.

GIRL: Well, let's talk about something else.

YOUNG MAN: Ok ... What shall we talk about, for example?

GIRL: I don't know ... What do you want to talk about?

YOUNG MAN: What would I like to talk about?

GIRL: Yeah, think about it ... [*still tidies up her stuff on the floor*]

YOUNG MAN: [*takes a bite out of the sandwich and thinks for a while*] So delicious ... thank you.

GIRL: Well, you love me, don't you? ... Sounds great!

YOUNG MAN: [*shocked*] What did you say?

GIRL: You love me very much, don't you?

YOUNG MAN: [*gets up and gives the sandwich to the* GIRL] What are you talking about? ... No one falls in love just with a sandwich, does he?

GIRL: [*takes the sandwich and is left helpless*] You said it was delicious, didn't you? ... I cooked it myself ... [*gives the sandwich to the* YOUNG MAN] Come on, have it ...

YOUNG MAN: Stop talking about these things.

GIRL: You accepted that we talk about something else.

YOUNG MAN: Ok ... it doesn't matter anymore. Say what you wish.

GIRL: I'd like to ask something if you don't mind.

YOUNG MAN: Never mind ... Ask it.

GIRL: What are you doing here?

YOUNG MAN: We're waiting for the law to be enforced!

GIRL: Aha, I see ... Will they torment you so much?

YOUNG MAN: Well, I should tolerate it ... It'll eventually pass over.

GIRL:	Yeah ... [*tidies up her stuff*] Since when have you been here?
YOUNG MAN:	I don't know ... It slipped my mind ... [*eats the last morsel*]
GIRL:	Like me ... Aww, how nice! ... I have my mirror here with me ...
YOUNG MAN:	What are you doing?
GIRL:	I'm looking at myself.
YOUNG MAN:	I'm talking about this stuff ... [*points at the ground cloth and other stuff*] What is all this?
GIRL:	Well, this is our living stuff.
YOUNG MAN:	What?! ... Our living stuff?
GIRL:	Aha ...
YOUNG MAN:	Pick them all up ... Here's not the right place to live ...
GIRL:	I know ... but I've travelled all around ... Here's a good place ... because there's someone who talks to me ... You can remind me of my name. You said you knew me.
YOUNG MAN:	Yeah, I did ... but here's not safe ... You don't know who come here ... My poor mother!
GIRL:	[*points at the stuff she put on the stage*] Look ... we've got everything needed for life.
YOUNG MAN:	What's that?
GIRL:	It's called a mirror.
YOUNG MAN:	Mirror! ... What's it good for?
GIRL:	It reflects your image ... [*holds out the mirror to the YOUNG MAN*] Come on ... You can look at yourself.
YOUNG MAN:	[*goes forward, gets the mirror from the GIRL, and looks at himself for a moment*] No ...!
GIRL:	It's the only thing I've had since before I began wandering around. It's still safe and sound.

YOUNG MAN:	Get it ... I don't want it.
GIRL:	What happened?
YOUNG MAN:	[*feels blue*] That wasn't me.
GIRL:	[*looks at her image in the mirror and smiles*] But it was ... but you didn't recognize it ... The mirror reflects anything as it is.
YOUNG MAN:	Impossible ... I didn't look like that ...
GIRL:	Like what ...?
YOUNG MAN:	How shall I know? ... That wasn't me anyway.
GIRL:	O'! ... Who was it then?
YOUNG MAN:	It was an odd and strange one whom I didn't recognize.
GIRL:	You think so ... My mirror reflects anything as it is.
YOUNG MAN:	No ... what I saw wasn't me.
GIRL:	Well, whom do they come to torture every day?
YOUNG MAN:	I don't know ... [*thoughtfully goes to sit on the pedestal like the sculpture by Rodin*] Who am I now?
GIRL:	[*lies down on the ground cloth and breathes a sigh of happiness*] Do you remember the last time I could sleep on the ground?
YOUNG MAN:	Maybe centuries ago ... Who was I then?
GIRL:	I wish I could stay here forever and get rid of that gadfly ... [*rolls around*] I wish I could stay here forever.
	The WOMAN *enters hastily and goes straight toward the* GIRL. *The* YOUNG MAN *is still thinking.*
WOMAN:	You again?! ... I knew you would show up again.
GIRL:	I was just passing by.
WOMAN:	You've always kept saying so ... Go away ...
GIRL:	I've been always right ... I have to pass by here every other time.

WOMAN:	The last time you came, I said you're no longer allowed to step in here.
GIRL:	Well, I've got nowhere to go but here …
WOMAN:	None of my business … You want to take my son away.
GIRL:	I've got nowhere to take him.
WOMAN:	[*messes up the* GIRL's *stuff*] Did you scatter them again? … Pick it all up and go away … Hurry up …
GIRL:	No … let me stay here.
WOMAN:	What is this junk then?
GIRL:	No … They'll be messed up.

The GIRL *tries to stop the* WOMAN. *The* WOMAN *makes her take her hand off. The mirror falls on the ground and breaks. The broken pieces scatter around the stage. Both stand still for a moment.*

GIRL:	My mirror … My mirror is broken!
WOMAN:	That's your own fault.
GIRL:	You broke my mirror.
WOMAN:	I told you to leave here … Why didn't you heed my words?
GIRL:	I thought that here …
WOMAN:	Here's not the right place for you … Got it? … Not the right place …
GIRL:	I'd got just one mirror … you broke it.
WOMAN:	But I didn't do it on purpose … [*gives a mirror to the* GIRL] Come on … Take my mirror instead.
GIRL:	[*takes the mirror and tries to clean it*] No … I want my own mirror.
WOMAN:	What's the difference? … This is a mirror too.
GIRL:	I don't want it … It's too blurry … It reflects nothing … Take it … [*gives the mirror back to the* WOMAN *and gets busy picking up her stuff*]

WOMAN: [*takes the mirror and looks at her image in a way
              that the audience can also see the blurred surface of
              the mirror which reflects nothing*] Right ... Maybe it's
              better this way.

GIRL: Shall I leave here now? ... I'm too tired.

WOMAN: [*tries to consoles the* GIRL] You don't understand,
              Girl ... Here is not the right place for you ... Look at
              me ... Please heed my words.

GIRL: [*folds up the ground cloth, takes a pack out of her
              backpack, and holds it to the* WOMAN] Take it ... I
              brought it for you.

WOMAN: What's that?

GIRL: Some food ... I cooked it myself.

WOMAN: No ... I've already had some ...

GIRL: Take and have it ... Your face has paled ... in hunger.

WOMAN: No ... it's because of food poisoning ... I can eat
              nothing anymore.

GIRL: Take it ... I cooked it for you.

WOMAN: [*takes the sandwich unwillingly*] You said my face
              has paled, didn't you?

GIRL: Aha ...

WOMAN: [*takes out her cosmetics hastily*] Well, I have to put
              on some more make-up then ... [*gets busy putting
              on make-up*]

GIRL: [*puts her stuff in her backpack*] If you didn't break
              my mirror ...

WOMAN: Go away ... [*wears rouge on her cheeks in an exag-
              gerated way*] I have to go too ... I can't keep them
              waiting more.

GIRL: [*points at the* YOUNG MAN] He ...

WOMAN: [*interrupts the* GIRL] He only has to think and you
              have to keep on travelling around too ... Now go ...

We're in trouble more than enough here. [*finishes with her make-up*]

The GIRL *looks at the* YOUNG MAN. *The* YOUNG MAN *calls after her as she walks a few steps further.*

YOUNG MAN: No ... Stay here.

GIRL: [*returns happily*] Shall I stay?! ... [*throws her back-pack on the floor*]

WOMAN: [*approaches the* GIRL] You don't know ... The time of vagrancy isn't over yet, Girl ...

The WOMAN *leaves the stage slowly and desperately. The* GIRL *notices the sandwich the* WOMAN *has left there.*

GIRL: [*picks it up*] She didn't take her sandwich ...

YOUNG MAN: She's got used to poisonous foods ...

GIRL: [*gets busy taking out her stuff enthusiastically and hurriedly*] How good will it be if I stay here forever.

YOUNG MAN: What do you mean?

GIRL: Wouldn't you like me to stay here then?

YOUNG MAN: I was thinking.

GIRL: Are you always busy thinking? [*spreads the ground cloth*]

YOUNG MAN: Yeah ... I have to.

GIRL: But I have to keep on going all the time. [*tidies up the stuff on the ground*]

YOUNG MAN: Where?

GIRL: I don't know ... I just know someone is following me and I have to go.

YOUNG MAN: But I have to think ... because when I said nonsense the first day, nobody noticed that they lacked something in their lives.

GIRL: What?

YOUNG MAN: Something that everybody has forgotten and lost.

GIRL: Well ... let's look for it.

YOUNG MAN: I myself don't know what it is.

GIRL: But I have everything you wish for here with me.

YOUNG MAN: [*moves on the stage and looks at the broken pieces of the mirror*] I should find it.

GIRL: Well, what are you looking for when you don't know what you've lost?

YOUNG MAN: I keep on searching to find it ... [*directs the* GIRL's *attention to one of the broken pieces of mirror*] Look ... It's my image that is mugging.

GIRL: For whom?

YOUNG MAN: For me ...

GIRL: No problem, I'll pick it up ... [*picks up the piece of mirror and looks at it*] Well, why isn't it mugging for me?

YOUNG MAN: I don't know ... [*turns back and shows her another piece of mirror*] Look at that one ...

GIRL: Is that one mugging for you too?

YOUNG MAN: No ... It shows me like a dinosaur.

GIRL: [*looks at the* YOUNG MAN] But you aren't a dinosaur, are you?

YOUNG MAN: I don't know ... Maybe I am.

GIRL: No ... I don't guess so ... I've seen some pictures of dinosaurs .... None of them looks like you ... [*picks up the piece of mirror*]

YOUNG MAN: Really?

GIRL: Yeah ... By the way, dinosaurs became extinct a long time ago ... You must have died by now if you were a dinosaur ... [*takes the* YOUNG MAN *to the other side*] Come here ... You don't need to look at them anymore ... [*throws the piece of mirror into the backpack*]

YOUNG MAN: [*points at the other broken pieces of the mirror*]
Those ... [*suffers from a morbid condition*]

GIRL: Are they all dinosaurs?

YOUNG MAN: I don't know ... [*stares at one of the broken pieces of mirror*] No ... [*turns his back*] Pick it up ...

GIRL: [*picks up the other piece of mirror hurriedly and throws it in the backpack too*] What was that?

YOUNG MAN: I didn't recognize it ... I've never seen it before.

GIRL: Was it so horrible?

YOUNG MAN: Yeah ... What did you do with it?

GIRL: [*doesn't take her hand out of the backpack*] Please ... Stop looking at them ...

YOUNG MAN: Who were they?

GIRL: I don't know ... I'm scared ... I feel cold whenever I fear.

YOUNG MAN: Well, stop being scared in order to not feel cold.

GIRL: [*cowers and squats on the matting*] I can't help it ... I fear when you're talking this way.

The YOUNG MAN *looks at the GIRL. Then he takes the torn and worn-out cloak from his shoulders and covers the* GIRL. *The* GIRL *fondles the cloak lovingly, holds it on her cheeks, and sniffs it. The* YOUNG MAN *walks around the stage with curiosity and looks at the broken pieces of mirror. He stands still suddenly.*

YOUNG MAN: Blood! ... There's blood on the ground ...

GIRL: No matter ... [*still holds her hand inside the backpack*]

YOUNG MAN: [*approaches the GIRL*] Is it your blood?

GIRL: I got flustered all of a sudden.

YOUNG MAN: Put out your hand and let me give it a look ...

GIRL: [*takes out her hand and tries to pretend she's happy by telling a joke*] Don't be sad ... That dinosaur bit it.

YOUNG MAN: Come on … Let me wrap it up.

GIRL: I have some bandage and medical plaster here with me … [*among the stuff scattered on the ground, she picks up the first aid kit and gives it to the* YOUNG MAN] Here it is … I said I've got everything needed here with me … [*The* YOUNG MAN *gets busy wrapping the bandage around her hand*] Why are looking like this?

YOUNG MAN: [*averts his eyes*] Nothing … your eyes.

GIRL: What's wrong with my eyes? … Ouch! … You don't need to look at the mirrors anymore …

YOUNG MAN: Are you warmed up now?

GIRL: Yeah … I feel cold whenever I fear …

YOUNG MAN: [*finishes wrapping the* GIRL's *hand*] Well, you shouldn't fear anymore. Ok?

GIRL: Ok … but when you're talking about those things …

YOUNG MAN: Hold up your hand to stop the bleeding … [*again goes to the mirrors and looks at his image*] Do you think there's anything stranger and more horrible than human beings? …

GIRL: [*cowers more tightly in the* YOUNG MAN's *cloak*] How warm and nice it is! … What about yourself then?

YOUNG MAN: Me?! … I don't know. I'm going to be scared.

GIRL: Well, are you going to feel cold now?

YOUNG MAN: No … I'm just scared … of them …

GIRL: Them …?!

The sound of an approaching train whistle is heard. At speed, the train passes in front of them. The YOUNG MAN *follows its route passing through the audience. The* GIRL *doesn't show any reaction. The* YOUNG MAN *follows the train's route a few steps further again and stops.*

YOUNG MAN: I told you so! … Another one again …

GIRL: [fondles the cloak] Yeah … We can go to a good place … I wouldn't like my son to be born here … [to the YOUNG MAN] What do you think about it?

YOUNG MAN: We can do nothing anymore …

GIRL: Yeah, I feel pity for him … I think … what's his fault that he will be born as a forgotten child? …

YOUNG MAN: [to himself] They all will die.

GIRL: But it doesn't matter. Instead, we'll be three rather than two … Then we could be four … We could be five too if we want … or … or even more …

YOUNG MAN: We'll increase in number day by day …

GIRL: We'll keep on increasing in number … so that we can fill all … It would be nice, wouldn't it?

YOUNG MAN: [still looking at the train's route] We should accept it … No way out.

GIRL: Right. Like the ancestors who were alone at first … Then … Then … [turns to the YOUNG MAN] What will happen next?

YOUNG MAN: All will go down a very deep valley … and die.

GIRL: Our children?!

YOUNG MAN: Which children …?

GIRL: Those who are going to be born.

YOUNG MAN: [confused] What are you talking about? … What will the children fill the world with?

GIRL: With themselves …

YOUNG MAN: What nonsense you say? … What do you mean by themselves?

GIRL: Well, you didn't heed my words, did you?

YOUNG MAN: Which words?

GIRL: Our children … Those who will increase in number day by day.

~47~

YOUNG MAN: Children?! … But we've got no children.

GIRL: We don't have any right now … but later.

YOUNG MAN: How's your hand?

GIRL: The bleeding has stopped … It's ok.

YOUNG MAN: [*Stares at the* GIRL.] I know … You're the one who has been lost.

GIRL: Me?! … But I'm here.

YOUNG MAN: Yeah … but you've been doomed to be vagrant and forgotten … Time will teach us anything in its new turn … We've had a vicious start … We should start again.

The YOUNG MAN *goes to sit on the pedestal like "The Thinker" sculpture.*

GIRL: [*lies down easily on the ground*] More than half the earth is left for me to finish with my vagrancy … I'm tired … tired.

The WOMAN *enters with a black eye, cuts and blood on her lips and in her mouth. Her dress is torn. She looks messy in appearance. She throws a glance at the* YOUNG MAN *and the* GIRL, *then sits downstage in the same place she sat at the beginning of the play like the portrait of Mona Lisa. She pauses for a while.*

WOMAN: I vomited … I vomited on them … [*looks at the* GIRL *for a few seconds and then turns back to the audience*] Poor Girl! … They want to invade love too … Well, go to sleep in order to resume your vagrancy tomorrow … till the day that is not known. You have to pay for your love and chastity … And until the last train passes along this railway, day by day I'm being poisoned more and more … and you'll happen to pass here and save my son with your love … That day is when you'll find your true name.

Final Curtain

www.ingramcontent.com/pod-product-compliance
Lightning Source LLC
LaVergne TN
LVHW011414080426
835511LV00005B/533